Simple to Sew Aprons

13 Sassy, Sweet & Functional Aprons in a Flash

by Billie Steward

LEISURE ARTS, INC. • Maumelle, Arkansas

Contents

Introduction 3
Bandanna Apron 4
Mommy & Me Aprons 10
Dishtowel Apron 16
Floral Delight Apron 20
Pinstripe Apron 24
Gardener's Apron 28
Cherry-O Apron............... 32
Sunflower Apron 36
Egg Gathering Apron......... 40
Red Stripe Apron.............. 44
Summer Picnic Apron......... 48
Harvest Apron 54
Retro Bib Apron............... 58
General Instructions 62
Meet Billie Steward........... 64

Introduction

Aprons are great for all the cooks in your life, whether they are professional, amateur, or even yourself. Make an apron for the man, the gardener, or the chicken lover in your life. Make a sweet matching mommy and daughter duo. Select the perfect apron for that perfect person and stitch up a quick and easy apron.

Bandanna Apron

Perfect for the chef in your life, this durable apron made of ticking fabric will protect your clothing but allow you to cook in style.

Shopping List

Yardage is based on 43"/44" (109 cm/112 cm) wide fabric with a usable width of 42" (107 cm).

» 2 yds (1.8 m) of ticking stripe fabric

» 1/2 yd (46 cm) of 7/8" (22 mm) wide bandanna print ribbon

» two 7/16" (11 mm) diameter grommets

» grommet setting tool

» water-soluble fabric marking pen

» coordinating sewing thread

» sheet of paper at least 15" x 15" (38 cm x 38 cm) for pattern

Cutting the Pieces

Follow Rotary Cutting, page 63, to cut fabric. Pieces can also be cut with a ruler or yardstick and scissors. Pay attention to the direction of the stripes when cutting pieces. All measurements include 1/2" seam allowances.

From ticking stripe fabric:

» Cut apron 30" x 36"

» Cut 2 waist ties 6" x 35"

» Cut neck tie 4" x 26"

» Cut pocket 10" x 15"

Making the Apron

*Follow **Machine Sewing**, page 63, to make apron. Match right sides and raw edges and use a 1/2" seam allowance unless otherwise indicated.*

1. To make pattern, cut paper to 15" x 15". Refer to **Fig. 1** to measure and mark 5 1/4" from top left corner and 12" from top right corner. Draw a line from point to point. Cut along drawn line.
2. Fold apron in half lengthwise. Pin pattern on corner of folded fabric with top edge of pattern even with top edge of apron. Draw along curved edge of pattern (**Fig. 2**). Cut out apron shape.
3. For bottom hem, press raw edge to wrong side 1/2"; press to wrong side 1/2" again. Stitch hem in place.
4. Repeat Step 3 for curved side hems and straight side hems.
5. For top hem, press raw edge to wrong side 1/2"; press to wrong side 1". Stitch hem in place.

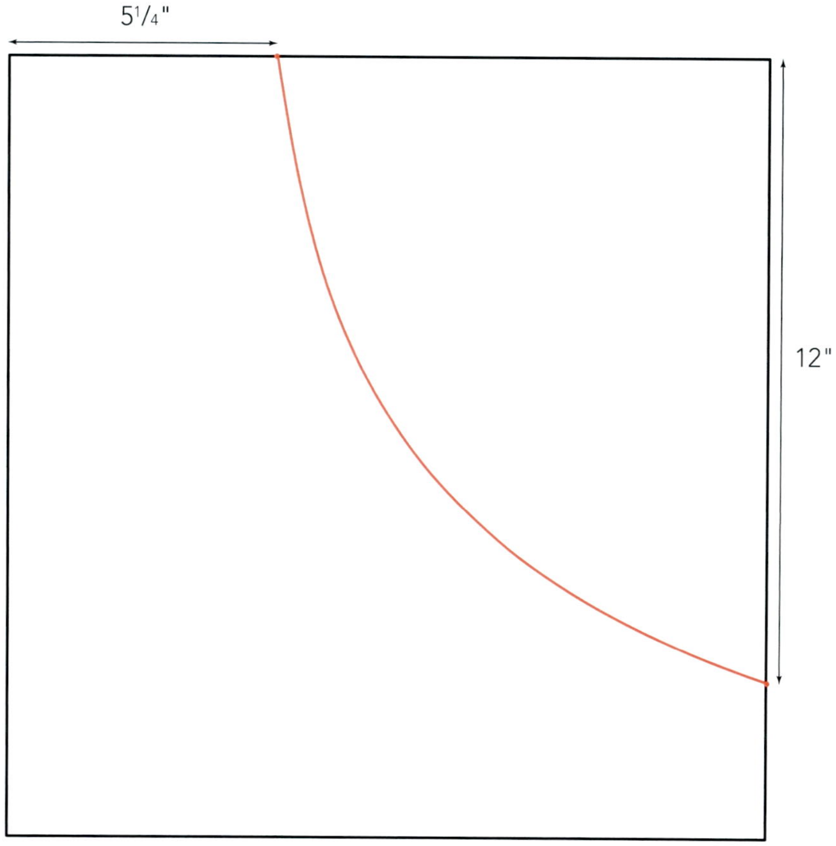

Fig. 1

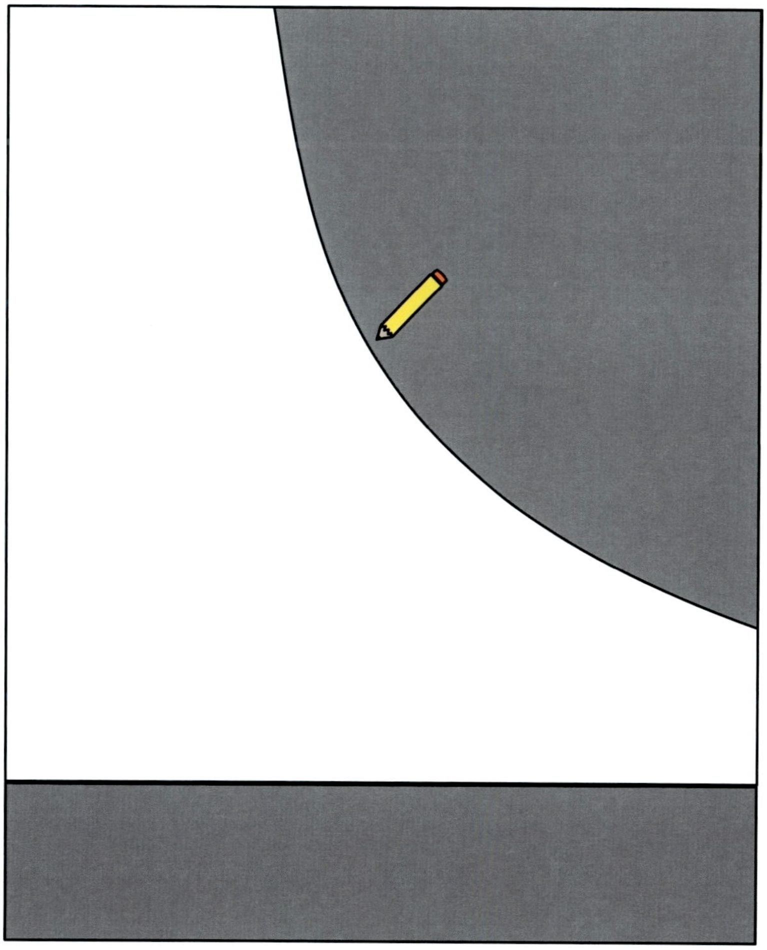

Fig. 2

6. For pocket, repeat Step 3 to hem each long edge and then each side edge.

7. Folding ends to wrong side even with sides of pocket, stitch ribbon to one long edge of pocket. Draw a line through center of pocket.

8. Center and pin pocket to apron with bottom edge of pocket 12 1/2" from bottom hem of apron. Stitch in place along sides and bottom. Stitch along drawn line.

9. For waist ties, press each short end to wrong side 1/2". Press ties in half lengthwise. Unfold and press each long raw edge to the creased center. With raw edges inside, press tie in half again. Stitch along folded edges. Stitch ties to sides of apron.

10. Repeat Step 9 for neck tie.

11. Follow manufacturer's instruction to install grommets at top corners of apron. Insert ends of neck tie through grommets back to front and knot to secure.

Mommy & Me Aprons

Nothing is more precious than time spent with your little "me" in the kitchen. And you'll both be ready for the task with your matching aprons.

SHOPPING LIST

Yardage given is for making both aprons. Yardage is based on 43"/44" (109 cm/112 cm) wide fabric with a usable width of 42" (107 cm).

- 2 yds (1.8 m) of floral print fabric
- 1¼ yds (1.1 m) of pink solid fabric
- 1 pkg extra-wide double-fold bias tape
- water-soluble fabric marking pen
- coordinating sewing thread
- sheet of paper at least 14" x 14" (36 cm x 36 cm) for adult apron pattern
- sheet of paper at least 10¼" x 14" (26 cm x 36 cm) for child's apron pattern

Cutting the Pieces

Follow Rotary Cutting, page 63, to cut fabric. Pieces can also be cut with a ruler or yardstick and scissors. Cut all strips from the selvage-to-selvage width of the fabric. All measurements include 1/2" seam allowances.

Adult Apron

From floral print fabric:

» Cut apron 28" x 32 1/2"

» Cut facing 2" x 13"

From pink solid fabric:

» Cut 2 waist ties 4" x 36"

» Cut 2 neck ties 4" x 22 1/2"

» Cut pocket 7" x 7 1/2"

Child's Apron

From floral print fabric:

» Cut apron 20 1/2" x 25 1/2"

» Cut facing 2" x 9"

From pink solid fabric:

» Cut 2 waist ties 4" x 26"

» Cut 2 neck ties 4" x 19"

» Cut pocket 5 1/2" x 6"

Making the Apron

Follow Machine Sewing, page 63, to make apron. Match right sides and raw edges and use a 1/2" seam allowance unless otherwise indicated.

Adult Apron

1. To make adult apron pattern, cut paper to 14" x 14". Refer to **Fig. 1** to measure and mark 7" from top left corner and 8 1/2" from top right corner. Draw a curved line from point to point. Cut along drawn line.
2. Fold apron in half lengthwise. Pin pattern on corner of folded fabric with top edge of pattern even with top edge of apron. Draw along curved edge of pattern **(Fig. 2)**. Cut out apron shape.
3. For bottom hem, press raw edge to wrong side 1/2"; press to wrong side 1/2" again. Stitch hem in place.
4. Repeat Step 3 for straight side hems and curved side hems.
5. For each neck tie, press one short end to wrong side 1/2". Press tie in half lengthwise. Unfold and press each long raw edge to the creased center. With raw edges inside, press tie in half again. Stitch along folded edges.
6. Baste each end of neck tie to top edge of apron approximately 3/8" from side edges.
7. Press each short edge of facing to wrong side 1/2"; press 1 long edge to wrong side. Sew facing to top of apron. Press facing to wrong side; topstitch in place.

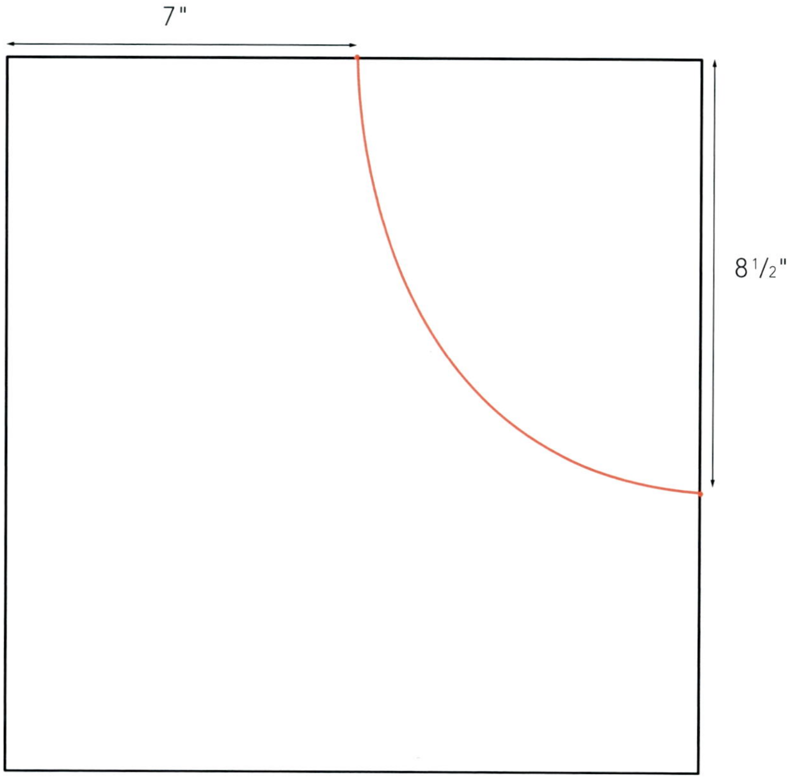

Fig. 1

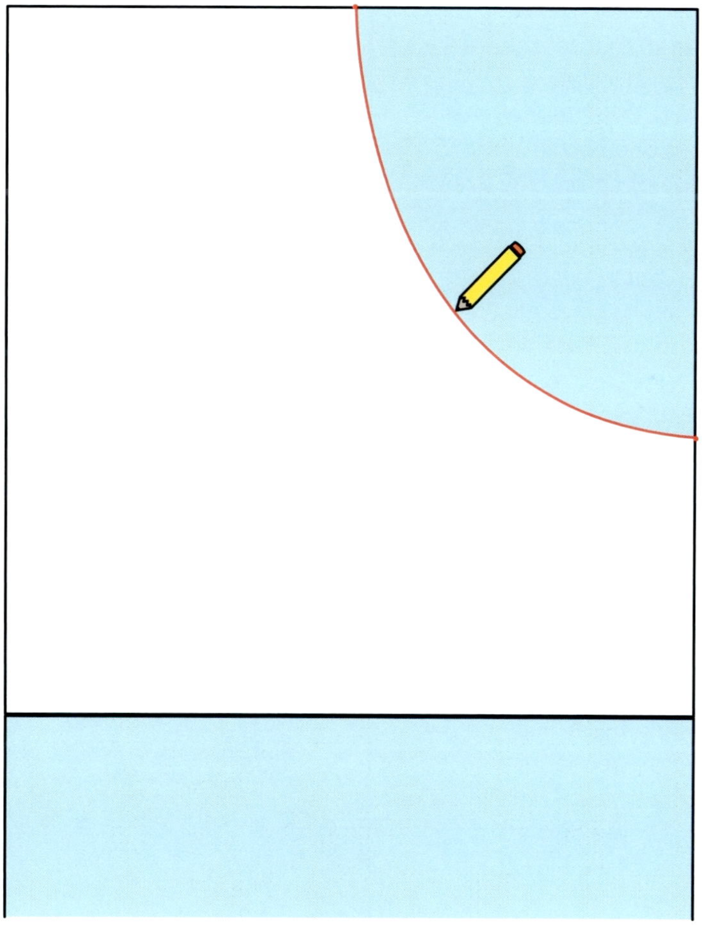

Fig. 2

8. For each waist tie, press each short end to wrong side $^{1}/_{2}$". Press ties in half lengthwise. Unfold and press each long raw edge to the creased center. With raw edges inside, press tie in half again. Stitch along folded edges. Stitch one end of each tie to each side of apron.

9. For pocket, encase top edge of pocket in bias tape. Stitch tape in place. Press remaining sides of pocket to wrong side $^{1}/_{2}$". Position pocket as desired; topstitch in place.

Child's Apron

1. To make child's apron pattern, cut paper to $10^{1}/_{4}$" x 14". Refer to **Fig. 3** to measure and mark 5" from top left corner and $7^{1}/_{2}$" from top right corner. Draw a curved line from point to point. Cut along drawn line.

2. Fold apron in half lengthwise. Pin pattern on corner of folded fabric with top edge of pattern even with top edge of apron. Draw along curved edge of pattern **(see Fig. 2)**. Cut out apron shape.

3. Repeat Steps 3-9 above to complete child's apron.

Fig. 3

Dishtowel Apron

Made from a cute checked dishtowel, this apron is super simple to sew and is incredibly functional.

SHOPPING LIST

Yardage is based on 43"/44" (109 cm/112 cm) wide fabric with a usable width of 42" (107 cm).

- 16" x 28" (41 cm x 71 cm) dishtowel
- 5/8 yd (57 cm) of coordinating fabric
- 7/8 yd (80 cm) of jumbo rickrack
- water-soluble fabric marking pen
- coordinating sewing thread

CUTTING THE PIECES

Follow Rotary Cutting, page 63, to cut fabric. Pieces can also be cut with a ruler or yardstick and scissors. Cut all strips from the selvage-to-selvage width of the fabric. All measurements include 1/2" seam allowances.

From coordinating fabric:

» Cut 2 ties 5" x width of fabric

» Cut 1 pocket 15" x 8"

Making the Apron

Follow Machine Sewing, page 63, to make apron. Match right sides and raw edges and use a 1/2" seam allowance unless otherwise indicated.

1. For pocket hem, press one long raw edge to wrong side 1/4"; press to wrong side 1/4" again. Stitch hem in place.
2. Press remaining raw edges 1/2" to wrong side. Draw a line through center of pocket.
3. Center and pin pocket to dishtowel with long, unhemmed edge (bottom) 3" from 1 long edge of dishtowel (bottom).
4. Slip rickrack under sides and bottom of pocket so that 1/2 of rickrack shows. Stitch pocket in place close to side and bottom edges. Sew along drawn line in center of pocket.
5. Cut 1 tie in half. Sew 1 half tie to each end of remaining tie to make 1 long tie.
6. Press all edges 1/2" to wrong side. Matching wrong sides and pressed edges, press tie in half.
7. Find center of tie and top center of dishtowel. Matching centers, place top of dishtowel 1/2" inside tie; pin. Topstitch close to all pressed edges.

Floral Delight Apron

A sprinkle of posies on a trellis background lends a Summer feel to this sweet bib apron.

SHOPPING LIST

Yardage is based on 43"/44" (109 cm/112 cm) wide fabric with a usable width of 42" (107 cm).

- 1 yd (91 cm) of print fabric
- 3/4 yd (69 cm) of gingham print fabric
- water-soluble fabric marking pen
- coordinating sewing thread

CUTTING THE PIECES

Follow Rotary Cutting, page 63, to cut fabric. Pieces can also be cut with a ruler or yardstick and scissors. Cut all strips from the selvage-to-selvage width of the fabric. All measurements include 1/2" seam allowances.

From print fabric:

- Cut apron skirt 17" x width of fabric
- Cut bib 12" x 13"

From gingham print fabric:

- Cut skirt trim 4" x width of fabric
- Cut 2 waist ties 7" x 35"
- Cut 2 neck ties 4" x 22"
- Cut bib trim 3" x 12"
- Cut facing 2" x 11"

Making the Apron

Follow Machine Sewing, page 63, to make apron. Match right sides and raw edges and use a 1/2" seam allowance unless otherwise indicated.

1. Sew skirt trim to apron skirt. Trim as needed if fabrics are not same width.
2. For bottom hem, press remaining long edge of trim to wrong side 1/2"; press to wrong side 1/2" again. Stitch hem in place. Repeat to hem apron skirt sides.
3. Baste 3/8" and again 1/8" from top edges of apron skirt. Pull top threads and gather apron skirt to measure 26" wide. Stitch 3/8" from edge to hold gathers in place.
4. Sew bib trim to top edge of bib. Follow Step 2 to hem bib sides.
5. Cut 1 waist tie in half. Sew 1 half waist tie to each end of remaining waist tie to make 1 long waist tie.
6. Press all edges 1/2" to wrong side. Matching wrong sides and pressed edges, press waist tie in half.
7. Find center of waist tie and top center of gathered apron skirt. Matching centers, sew gathered edge of apron skirt to 1 edge of waist tie.
8. Find center of bib bottom. Matching centers, sew bib bottom to remaining long edge of waist tie.
9. Matching wrong sides and pressed edges, fold waist tie, covering gathered edge. ***(Note:** At this point bib is facing toward bottom of apron skirt.)*
10. Fold bib up so that bib is facing right side up; pin. Topstitch close to all pressed edges, continuing along folded edge of waist tie to hold bib in place.
11. For each neck tie, press 1 short end 1/2" to wrong side. Press tie in half lengthwise. Unfold and press each long raw edge to the creased center. With raw edges inside, press tie in half again. Stitch along folded edges.
12. Baste end of each neck tie to top edge of apron approximately 1" from side edges.
13. For apron facing, press 1 long raw edge to wrong side 1/2". Matching right sides, sew facing to apron center top with neck ties sandwiched in between. Press facing to wrong side of apron. Topstitch 1" from top edge of facing.

Pinstripe Apron

Steal your husband's shirt from his closet and reinvent it. Give it some whimsical buttons and decorative trim and you'll be sporting a new apron in no time. Just don't steal his best shirt!

SHOPPING LIST

Yardage is based on 43"/44" (109 cm/112 cm) wide fabric with a usable width of 42" (107 cm).

- Men's shirt - size XL
- 1/2 yd (46 cm) of fabric for binding
- two assorted 7/16" (11 mm) buttons
- six assorted 1/2" (13 mm) buttons
- 1/2" (13 mm) bias tape maker (optional)
- coordinating sewing thread
- water-soluble fabric marking pen

CUTTING THE PIECES

Follow Rotary Cutting, page 63, to cut fabric. Pieces can also be cut with a ruler or yardstick and scissors. All measurements include 1/2" seam allowances.

From binding fabric:

- Cut 2 waist ties 4" x 36" across the width of the fabric
- For bias binding, cut 2" wide bias strips from remaining fabric to total approximately 110" when sewn together.

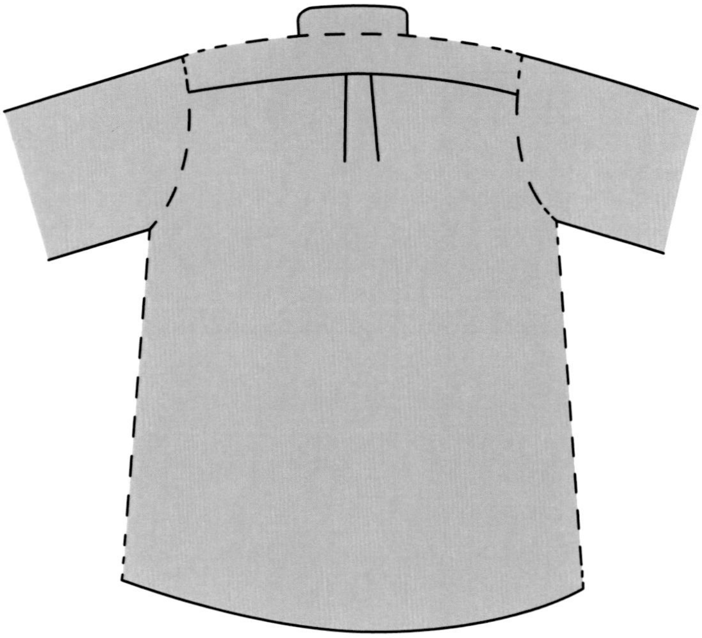

Fig. 1

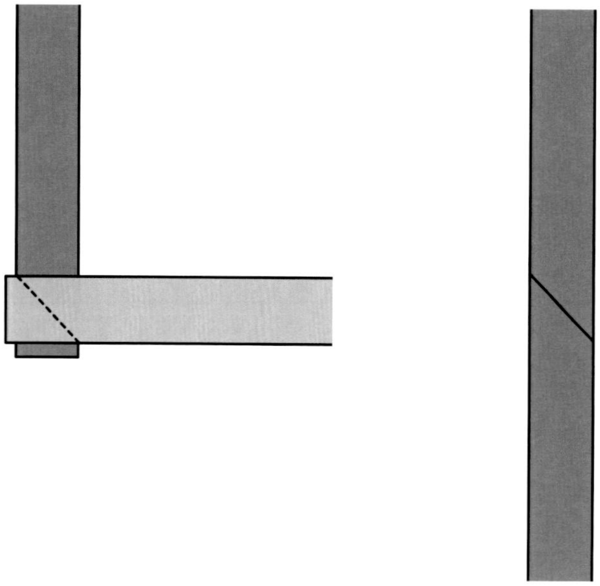

Fig. 2

Making the Apron

Follow Machine Sewing, page 63, to make apron. Use a 1/2" seam allowance unless otherwise indicated.

1. With shirt buttoned and back facing up, lay shirt flat on work surface. Refer to **Fig. 1** to cut sleeves from shirt. Cut along side seams. Cut straight across each shoulder to collar band. Cut around back of collar as close to lower edge of collar band as possible. At this point you should only have shirt fronts with collar attached. Discard shirt back and sleeves.
2. To angle side of apron, draw a line from top of shoulder to just below armhole. Repeat for other side of shirt front.
3. Pin button placket closed. Remove buttons from shirt; discard. Beginning at 3rd buttonhole from top (including neckband buttonhole), sew placket closed along previous stitching line, stopping about 1" from bottom and leaving top portion open to allow for apron to ease over head.
4. Sew bias strips together end to end using a diagonal seam (**Fig. 2**).
5. To make binding, press bias strip in half lengthwise. Unfold and press each long raw edge to the creased center. With raw edges inside, press bias strip in half again. **Option:** You can also use a bias tape maker to fold and press bias binding.
6. Encase bottom edge of 1 shirt front in binding, folding raw edge of binding to wrong side at placket edge and leaving unfolded at side edge. Stitch binding in place.
7. Repeat for bottom edge of remaining shirt front.
8. Repeat for each side edge, folding raw edge of binding to wrong side at bottom edge and leaving unfolded at top edge.
9. Repeat for top edge (along angled edges and around neckline), folding raw edges of binding to wrong side at beginning and end.
10. To make each waist tie, press each short end to wrong side 1/2". Press ties in half lengthwise. Unfold and press each long raw edge to the creased center. With raw edges inside, press tie in half again. Sew along folded edges. Sew ties to sides of apron.
11. Using smaller buttons for collar, sew assorted button at each buttonhole.

Gardener's Apron

Gardening is wonderful but can get down right dirty! Sometimes you need a bit of protection for your clothing. And this handy apron provides lots of pockets to carry your pruners and shears.

SHOPPING LIST

Yardage is based on 43"/44" (109 cm/112 cm) wide fabric with a usable width of 42" (107 cm).

- 7/8 yd (80 cm) of print fabric
- 1 yd (91 cm) of denim fabric
- water-soluble fabric marking pen
- coordinating sewing thread

CUTTING THE PIECES

Follow Rotary Cutting, page 63, to cut fabric. Pieces can also be cut with a ruler or yardstick and scissors. Cut all strips from the selvage-to-selvage width of the fabric. All measurements include 1/2" seam allowances.

From print fabric:

» Cut apron body front 22" x 17"

» Cut pocket 22" x 9 1/2"

From denim fabric:

» Cut 2 ties 36" x 2"

» Cut apron body back 22" x 17"

» Cut pocket 22" x 12"

Making the Apron

Follow Machine Sewing, page 63, to make apron. Matching right sides and raw edges and use a $^1/_2$" seam allowance unless otherwise indicated.

1. To hem denim pocket, press 1 long raw edge to wrong side $^1/_2$"; press to wrong side $^1/_2$" again. Stitch hem in place.

2. Repeat Step 1 to hem 1 long edge of print pocket. Mark 2 stitching lines 7$^1/_2$" from each short raw edge.

3. Matching side and bottom raw edges, stack print pocket on top of denim pocket; baste in place. Stitch along drawn lines to form pocket dividers.

4. For each tie, press one short edge and each long edge $^1/_2$" to wrong side. Matching wrong sides and pressed edges, press tie in half. Stitch along all pressed edges.

5. Matching right sides and raw edges, pin 1 tie to each side edge of apron body front $^5/_8$" below top raw edge; baste in place.

6. With ties sandwiched in between, sew apron body front to apron body back, leaving an opening for turning. Turn apron right side out; press. Topstitch along all apron body edges, sewing opening closed.

Cherry-O Apron

This apron will take you back to yesteryear with its sweet cherry print. It may even inspire you to make a cherry pie.

SHOPPING LIST

Yardage is based on 43"/44" (109 cm/112 cm) wide fabric with a usable width of 42" (107 cm).

- 5/8 yd (57 cm) of print fabric
- 1/4 yd (23 cm) of gingham check fabric
- 76" (193 cm) of 1 1/2" (38 mm) wide gingham ribbon (I used wire-edge ribbon and removed the wire)
- water-soluble fabric marking pen
- coordinating sewing thread

CUTTING THE PIECES

Follow Rotary Cutting, page 63, to cut fabric. Pieces can also be cut with a ruler or yardstick and scissors. Cut all strips from the selvage-to-selvage width of the fabric. All measurements include 1/2" seam allowances.

From print fabric:

» Cut apron body 19" x width of fabric

From gingham check fabric:

» Cut 2 pockets 7" x 7"

Making the Apron

Follow Machine Sewing, page 63, to make apron. Match right sides and raw edges and use a 1/2" seam allowance unless otherwise indicated.

1. For bottom hem, press long raw edge of apron body to wrong side 1/2"; press to wrong side 1/2" again. Stitch hem in place.
2. Repeat Step 1 to hem top and sides of apron body.
3. Repeat Step 1 to hem 1 edge of pocket. Press remaining edges 1/2" to wrong side. Repeat for remaining pocket. Set pockets aside.
4. Refer to **Fig. 1** to fold and press 2" pleats from top to bottom as indicated. Baste pleats in place across top edge.
5. Position pockets in center of apron body with top corners of pockets 4 1/4" from top and bottom corners 3" apart. Topstitch pockets along side and bottom edges.
6. Center ribbon along top of apron and topstitch in place along top and bottom edges.

Fig. 1

Sunflower Apron

This bright and bold sunflower apron will bring sunshine to your everyday cooking taskes.

SHOPPING LIST

Yardage is based on 43"/44" (109 cm/112 cm) wide fabric with a usable width of 42" (107 cm).

» 1/2 yd (46 cm) of sunflower print fabric

» 1/2 yd (46 cm) of coordinating print fabric

» water-soluble fabric marking pen

» coordinating sewing thread

CUTTING THE PIECES

Follow Rotary Cutting, page 63, to cut fabric. Pieces can also be cut with a ruler or yardstick and scissors. Cut all strips from the selvage-to-selvage width of the fabric. All measurements include 1/2" seam allowances.

From sunflower print fabric:

» Cut apron body 28" x 13 1/2"

From coordinating print fabric:

» Cut 2 ties 6" x width of fabric

» Cut apron trim 28" x 5"

Making the Apron

Follow Machine Sewing, page 63, to make apron. Match right sides and raw edges and use a $^1/_2$" seam allowance unless otherwise indicated.

1. Sew apron trim to apron body.
2. For bottom hem, press long raw edge of trim to wrong side $^1/_2$"; press to wrong side $^1/_2$" again. Stitch hem in place.
3. Repeat Step 2 to hem sides of apron.
4. Cut 1 tie in half. Sew 1 half tie to each end of remaining tie to make 1 long tie.
5. Press all edges $^1/_2$" to wrong side. Matching wrong sides and pressed edges, press tie in half.
6. Find center of tie and top center of apron body. Matching centers, place top of apron body $^1/_2$" inside tie; pin. Topstitch close to all pressed edges.

Egg Gathering Apron

Do you have chickens in your backyard? This apron is an oh-so-cute alternative to a basket for gathering your eggs. And this apron will keep your eggs safe and secure while you do your other chores - like feeding and watering.

SHOPPING LIST

Yardage is based on 43"/44" (109 cm/112 cm) wide fabric with a usable width of 42" (107 cm).

- $^1/_2$ yd (46 cm) of print fabric
- $1^1/_2$ yds (1.4 m) of dot print fabric
- water-soluble fabric marking pen
- coordinating sewing thread

CUTTING THE PIECES

Follow Rotary Cutting, page 63, to cut fabric. Pieces can also be cut with a ruler or yardstick and scissors. Cut all strips from the selvage-to-selvage width of the fabric. All measurements include 1/2" seam allowances.

From print fabric:

» Cut apron body 30" x 16"

From dot print fabric:

» Cut 2 pockets 6" x 51 1/2"

» Cut 2 ties 4" x 40"

Making the Apron

Follow Machine Sewing, page 63, to make apron. Match right sides and raw edges and use a 1/2" seam allowance unless otherwise indicated.

1. For bottom hem, press long raw edge of apron body to wrong side 1/2"; press to wrong side 1/2" again. Stitch hem in place.
2. Repeat Step 1 to hem sides of apron body.
3. To hem top edge of each egg pocket, press 1 long raw edge of pocket to wrong side 1/2"; press to wrong side 1/2" again. Stitch hem in place. Press remaining edges 1/2" to wrong side.
4. Refer to **Fig. 1** to fold and press pleats as indicated.
5. Center 1 pocket 2 1/2" above bottom edge of apron body. Stitch pocket in place along side and bottom edges.
6. Repeat Step 4 for remaining pocket.
7. Center pocket 1 1/2" above lower pocket. Stitch pocket in place along sides and bottom edges.
8. Draw a line through the center of each 4 1/2" area. Stitch along drawn line.
9. Cut 1 tie in half. Sew 1 half tie to each end of remaining tie to make 1 long tie.
10. Press all edges 1/2" to wrong side. Matching wrong sides and pressed edges, press tie in half.
11. Find center of tie and top center of apron body. Matching centers, place top of apron body 1/2" inside tie; pin. Topstitch close to all pressed edges.

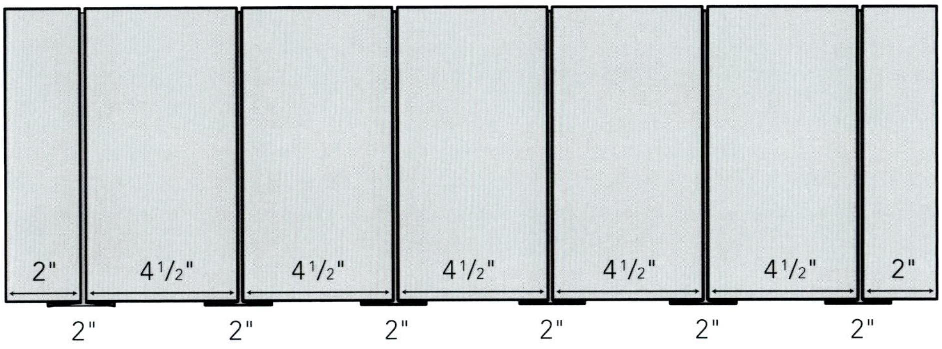

Fig. 1

Red Stripe Apron

Made from a great red and white stripe fabric, this basic apron is a must-have for every kitchen.

SHOPPING LIST

Yardage is based on 43"/44" (109 cm/112 cm) wide fabric with a usable width of 42" (107 cm).

- 1 yd (91 cm) of stripe fabric
- $3\frac{1}{4}$ yds (3 m) of 1" (25 cm) twill tape
- two $\frac{7}{16}$" (11 mm) diameter grommets
- grommet setting tool
- water-soluble fabric marking pen
- coordinating sewing thread

PENNE
MADE IN ITALY

CUTTING THE PIECES

Follow Rotary Cutting, page 63, to cut fabric. Pieces can also be cut with a ruler or yardstick and scissors. Pay attention to the direction of the stripes when cutting pieces. All measurements include 1/xx" seam allowances.

From stripe fabric:

- Cut apron 30" x 33"
- Cut pocket 7 1/2" x 9"

Making the Apron

Follow Machine Sewing, page 63, to make apron.

1. Fold apron in half lengthwise. Refer to **Fig. 1** to mark and cut shape of apron.
2. For bottom hem, press raw edge to wrong side 1/2"; press to wrong side 1/2" again. Stitch hem in place.
3. Repeat Step 2 for straight side hems and angled side hems.
4. For top hem, press raw edge to wrong side 1/2"; press to wrong side 1 1/2". Stitch hem in place.
5. Follow manufacturer's instructions to attach grommets at top corners and at top side edges.
6. For pocket, repeat Step 2 to hem 1 long edge. Press side and bottom edges 1/2" to wrong side. Draw a line 1 1/2" from right edge.
7. Center and pin pocket to apron 4" from top edge of apron. Topstitch along side and bottom edges. Stitch along drawn line.
8. Cut twill tape in half. Insert end of 1 length through 1 top grommet from front to back. Fold end 1/2" to wrong side and stitch to secure about 1 1/2" from grommet center. Repeat with remaining twill tape length in remaining grommet.
9. Press end of 1 twill tape length 1/2" to wrong side. Press 1/2" to wrong side again; topstitch in place. Repeat for remaining length.
10. Criss-cross twill tape and feed through waist grommets from back to front.

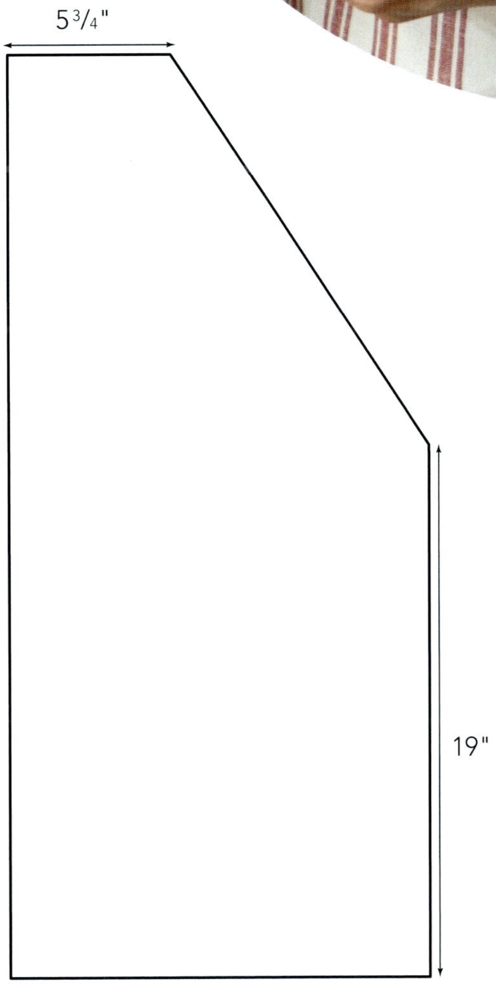

Fig. 1

Summer Picnic Apron

Enjoy the warm days of summer with this apron made from a men's shirt. Perfect for a picnic or cookout, this apron sports it's own collar and rickrack along the placket.

SHOPPING LIST

Yardage is based on 43"/44" (109 cm/112 cm) wide fabric with a usable width of 42" (107 cm).

- » Men's shirt - size XL
- » 1 pkg extra-wide double-fold bias tape
- » 1 yd (91 cm) of jumbo rickrack
- » coordinating sewing thread

MAKING the Apron

Follow Machine Sewing, page 63, to make apron. Use a 1/2" seam allowance unless otherwise indicated.

1. With shirt buttoned and back facing up, lay shirt flat on work surface. Refer to **Fig. 1** to cut sleeves from shirt. Cut along side seams. Cut straight across each shoulder to collar band. Cut around collar as close to lower edge of collar band as possible. At this point you should have shirt fronts, shirt back, collar (with collar band attached), and sleeves.

2. From shirt back (and sleeves, if needed), cut as many 4" wide strips as needed to make 2 waist ties 36" long and 1 neck tie 23" long. Cut facing 2 1/2" x 12 3/4"; set aside. Sew 4" wide strips together end to end and cut to length for waist ties and neck tie.

3. Referring to **Fig. 2**, measure 14" from side bottom of shirt; mark. Center placket and draw a straight line across upper edge of shirt where collar was removed so that it measures 11 3/4" wide. Draw a line from mark to mark at each side. Cut along drawn lines.

4. Pin button placket closed. Place rickrack under button placket edge. Catching rickrack in stitching and folding raw edge of rickrack under at ends, sew placket closed along previous stitching line.

5. For neck tie, press tie in half lengthwise. Unfold and press each long raw edge to the creased center. With raw edges inside, press tie in half again. Stitch along folded edges.

6. Pin short raw ends of neck tie on right side at top of apron 3/4" from each side adjusting length as desired; baste in place.

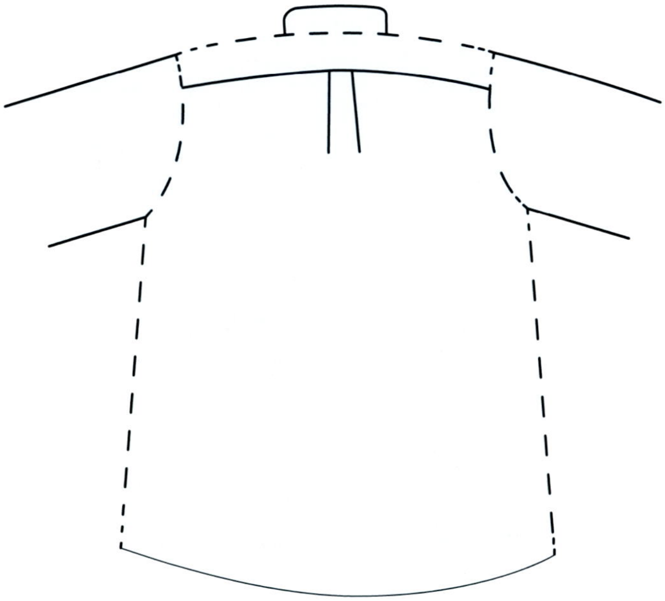

Fig. 1

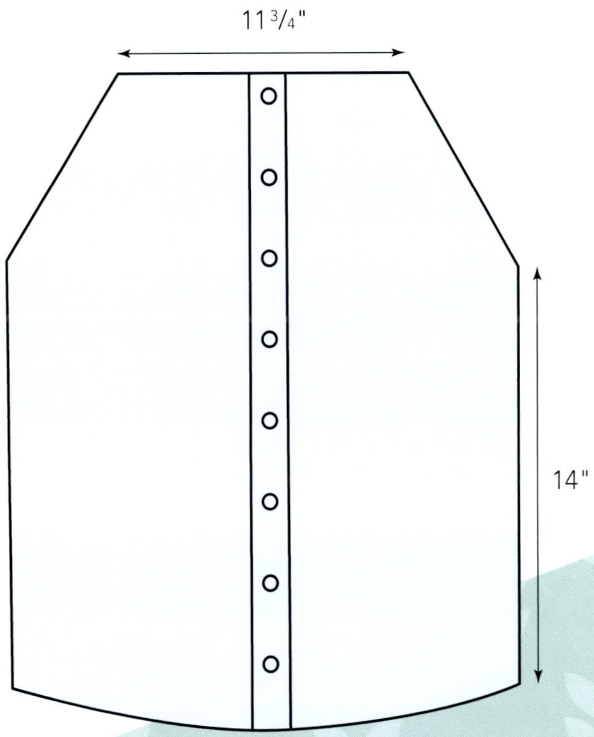

Fig. 2

7. For apron facing, press 1 long edge and each short end 1/2" to wrong side. Sew 1 long edge to top of apron. Press facing to wrong side of apron. Stitch facing in place about 1 1/4" from top edge.

8. Encase each side edge of apron in bias tape, folding raw edge of bias tape to wrong side at bottom edge and leaving unfolded at top edge.

9. With collar folded up out of the way, center collar band along top edge of apron; pin. Stitch collar band in place along top and bottom edges. Turn collar down and trim ends of collar and band even with edges of apron.

10. To make each waist tie, press each short end to wrong side 1/2". Press ties in half lengthwise. Unfold and press each long raw edge to the creased center. With raw edges inside, press tie in half again. Sew along folded edges. Sew ties to sides of apron.

11. Encase each angled edge of apron in bias tape, folding raw edges of bias tape to wrong edge at each end and catching ends of collar in binding.

Harvest Apron

This apron makes it so simple to gather and carry your garden harvest. Your hands are free for picking and gathering and the ample pouch holds a bountiful crop.

SHOPPING LIST

Yardage is based on 43"/44" (109 cm/112 cm) wide fabric with a usable width of 42" (107 cm).

- 1 yd (91 cm) of bandanna print fabric
- $1^{3}/_{8}$ yds (1.3 m) of patchwork bandanna print fabric
- 1" (25 mm) diameter button to cover
- 24" (61 cm) of $^{1}/_{2}$" (13 mm) wide elastic
- water-soluble fabric marking pen
- coordinating sewing thread
- large safety pin

CUTTING THE PIECES

Follow Rotary Cutting, page 63, to cut fabric. Pieces can also be cut with a ruler or yardstick and scissors. Cut all strips from the selvage-to-selvage width of the fabric. All measurements include 1/2" seam allowances.

From bandanna print fabric:

» Cut apron 31" x width of fabric

» Cut button loop 1/2" x 5"

From patchwork bandanna print fabric:

» Cut apron lining 31" x width of fabric

» Cut 2 ties 7" x width of fabric

Making the Apron

Follow Machine Sewing, page 63, to make apron. Match right sides and raw edges and use a 1/2" seam allowance unless otherwise indicated.

1. For button loop, press edges 1/8" to wrong side; topstitch along each pressed edge.
2. Find center of 1 long edge of apron; mark. Baste ends of button loop where marked.
3. Sew apron to apron lining along edge with loop attached and each short edge. Turn apron right side out; press.
4. To gather apron, baste 3/8" and again 1/8" from raw edges. Pull top threads and gather apron to measure 24" wide. Stitch 3/8" from edge to hold gathers in place.
5. Cut 1 tie in half. Sew 1 half tie to each end of remaining tie to make 1 long tie. Trim tie to measure 75".
6. Press all edges 1/2" to wrong side. Matching wrong sides and pressed edges, press tie in half.
7. Find center of tie and top center of gathered apron. Matching centers, place top of apron 1/2" inside tie; pin. Topstitch close to all pressed edges.
8. To make elastic casing, stitch 3/4" from bottom edge of apron. Use a seam ripper to open side seams of casing area. Attach a safety pin to 1 end of elastic. Use safety pin to work elastic through casing, pinning ends of elastic at each end of casing. Stitch casing closed, securing elastic.
9. Fold bottom of apron to front, forming pouch. Topstitch sides of pouch closed.
10. Follow manufacturer's instructions to cover button. Sew button to center of tie.

Retro Bib Apron

This apron is reminiscent of the women in your life and your connections to them. But in these modern bold fabrics, it will be your go-to apron for preparing every meal.

SHOPPING LIST

Yardage is based on 43"/44" (109 cm/112 cm) wide fabric with a usable width of 42" (107 cm).

- 1/2 yd (46 cm) of large print fabric for apron center [If using a directional print, you will need 1 yd (91 cm)]
- 1 yd (91 cm) of small print fabric for sides, pockets, neck tie, and waist ties
- 2 packages (6 yds) of extra-wide double-fold bias tape
- water-soluble fabric marking pen
- coordinating sewing thread

CUTTING THE PIECES

Follow Rotary Cutting, page 63, to cut fabric. Pieces can also be cut with a ruler or yardstick and scissors. Cut all strips from the selvage-to-selvage width of the fabric. All measurements include ½" seam allowances.

From large print fabric:

» Cut apron center 13" x 32"

» Cut apron facing 2½" x 13"

From small print fabric:

» Cut 2 apron sides 9" x 18"

» Cut 2 apron pockets 11" x 7"

» Cut 2 waist ties 6" x 35"

» Cut neck tie 4" x 23"

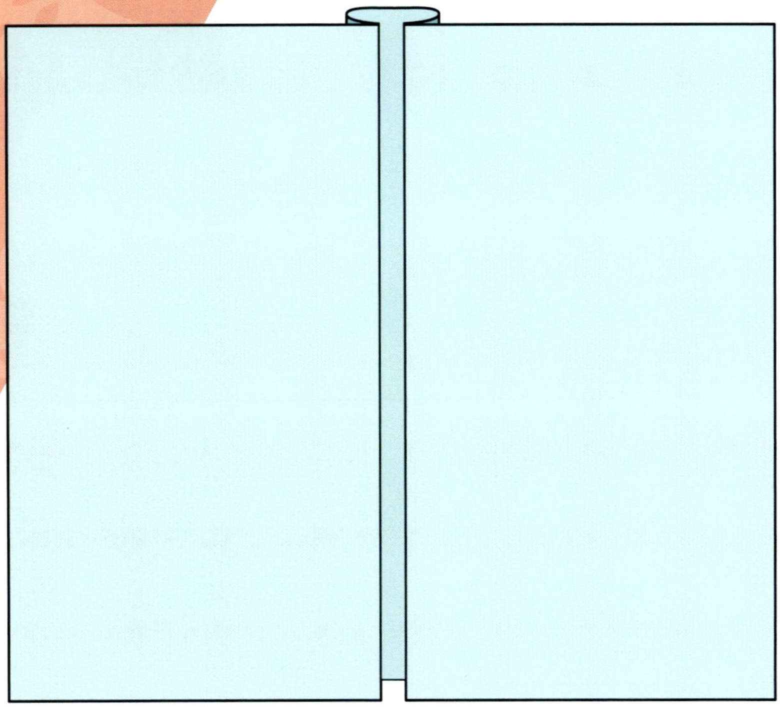

Fig. 1

Making the Apron

Follow Machine Sewing, page 63, to make apron. Match right sides and raw edges and use a 1/2" seam allowance unless otherwise indicated.

1. For pocket hem, press 1 long raw edge to wrong side 1/2"; press to wrong side 1/2" again. Stitch hem in place.
2. Mark center of opposite long raw edge. Pleat bottom edge of pocket at center mark so that pocket measures 9" wide (**Fig. 1**); press. Baste pleat in place.
3. Encase bottom edge of pocket in bias tape. Stitch tape in place.
4. Pin pocket to 1 apron side 4" from one short edge and with side edges even. Baste side edges in place. Topstitch bottom of pocket in place close to edge of bias tape.
5. Encase top edge of apron side in bias tape. Stitch tape in place.
6. Repeat Steps 1-5 for remaining pocket and apron side.
7. Matching bottom edges, sew apron sides to apron center.
8. For neck tie, press tie in half lengthwise. Unfold and press each long raw edge to the creased center. With raw edges inside, press tie in half again. Stitch along folded edges.
9. Pin short raw ends of neck tie on right side at top of apron center 3/4" from each side adjusting length as desired; baste in place.
10. For apron facing, sew 1 long edge to top of apron center. Press facing to wrong side of apron. Press raw edge of facing 1" to wrong side. Stitch facing in place about 1" from top edge.
11. Encase apron center sides, apron bottom, and apron sides in bias tape. Stitch tape in place.
12. For ties, repeat Step 8, pressing short ends 1/2" to wrong side before pressing ties lengthwise.
13. Sew apron ties to sides of apron.

General Instructions

Selecting Fabrics

Choose high-quality, medium-weight 100% cotton fabrics. Yardage requirements for cotton fabrics listed are based on 43"/44" wide fabric with a "usable" width of 40" after shrinkage and trimming selvages. Actual usable width will probably vary slightly from fabric to fabric.

Preparing Fabrics

Fabrics should be washed, dried, and pressed before cutting. Prepare cotton fabrics with a steam iron set on cotton and starch or sizing. The starch or sizing will give the fabric a crisp finish. This will make cutting more accurate and may make sewing easier.

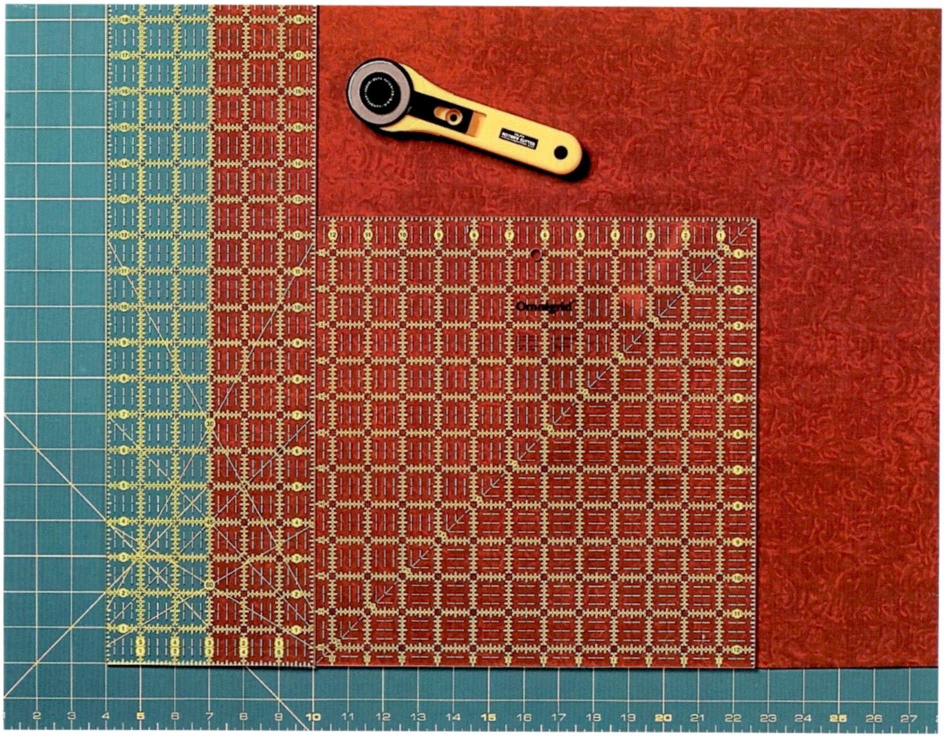

Fig. 1

Fig. 2

Rotary Cutting

- Place fabric on work surface with fold closest to you.
- Cut all strips from the selvage-to-selvage width of the fabric unless otherwise indicated in project instructions.
- Square left edge of fabric using rotary cutter and rulers **(Figs. 1-2)**
- To cut each strip required for a project, place ruler over cut edge of fabric, aligning desired marking on ruler with cut edge; make cut **(Fig. 3)**.

Fig. 3

Machine Sewing

Precise cutting, followed by accurate sewing, will ensure that all pieces of the project fit together well.

- Set sewing machine stitch length for approximately 11 stitches per inch.
- Use general-purpose sewing thread in needle and in bobbin.
- An accurate seam allowance is important.

Billie Steward

Billie Steward enjoys sewing "anything for the home" but says pillows and custom-fit slipcovers are her favorite projects.

"About 17 years ago, I was asked by an interior designer friend if I would make a few pillows for a client of hers. Of course, I said yes, and that job led to another which then led to my custom slipcover business."

But Billie's design talent is not limited to sewing for the home. Billie has the gift of imagining an endless array of projects using fabrics and other media.

A former designer and technical writer for Leisure Arts, Billie says she received her love for design and her ability to create what she sees in her mind from her mother.

Her designs have appeared in several Arkansas home decorating and lifestyle magazines.

Billie has designed other books for Leisure Arts, including #7188 *Make Your Own Quiet Book*, #7219 *Fidget to Focus*, #7220 *Tuffets & Poufs*, #7324 *Home Décor Using Grommets*, #7569 *Jelly Roll Rugs & More* and #7570 *Beat the Chill*.

Billie spends her spare time doting on her four cats or relaxing at nearby Greer's Ferry Lake.

Library of Congress Control Number: 2019914117

Made in U.S.A.

Production Team: Technical Editor – Lisa Lancaster; Graphic Designer – Kate Moul, Photography Stylist – Lori Wenger; Photographer – Jason Masters.